The Subtle Art Of Evolving

Become The Greatest Version Of Yourself

Derek J. Kenmuir

This book is dedicated to YOU!!!

P.s. I am a little mean in this book – If you get offended it only means what I said worked.

First Edition: (TBA Year & Month)
Printed in the United States of America
ISBN: [ISBN number with hyphens]

TABLE OF CONTENTS

Preface

Life is not a game. You get one. If you die there is no coming back. I almost died and that is one main reason why I am writing this book. To help you achieve unbelievable success and to leave a legacy worth talking about for generations to follow.

Let me share that moment and take you back in time. On Feb 26, 2006, I was twenty years old. Feeling untouchable, why, because up to this moment I had never lost a fight and never ever had my life change in an instant like it did on this day. If you ever been downtown Vancouver, British Columbia, Canada, you would be familiar with this area. I was about thirty feet or so away from the main entrance of the International Village Mall. Not the greatest area in our beautiful city, but I was there. Waiting for a friend to show up, we had the initial plan to catch up and watch a movie since we haven't seen one another since High School. That plan didn't happen. What did happen even God himself couldn't predict. I looked down at my watch to check the time. It was 1:03 pm. I remember because that meant my friend was thirty-three minutes late. The next thing I heard altered my life. *Nice Watch!* I didn't get a chance to look up. I didn't get a chance to react. I didn't get a chance to do anything, a big old nothing. Four drug addicted individuals bonded together. Why? To get my watch to sell or trade for drugs, can you believe that? One of these elite members of society took a switchblade and stabbed me right in the bloody head. Literally inches away from my right eye, too close for comfort if you ask me. Everything went blurry and then black fast. Regaining consciences I couldn't focus correctly. All I could do was watch the stone cold concrete get closer and closer and closer as my whole now deadweight body tumbled to the ground. The experts say when you have a life-death situation your life flashes through your eyes, do you agree? I didn't see anything. Not a single thing. To this moment of my life, I never achieved anything. It was blank. Totally blank, pitch dark black, it is like I blinked and a fast second later I was face down on the cement. Twenty years old and I was about to die. I was about to die with nothing, absolutely a big old nothing. Blood was now gushing out my head. Not only could I feel it, but I could taste it as it ran down the side of my face and right into my mouth. I was frozen. I couldn't move. Possible paralyzed or petrified. All I could hear myself do was struggle for my next breath as I managed to lift myself inches off the ground. When I did that I witnessed my vital fluid stain the concrete below me. It was like watching a horror movie, but it real life and I was scared shitless. It wasn't over. The gentlemen that initiated the attack must have been on something good. I say that as he saw me in my new helpless state and decided quickly I might add to step up his game. Not knowing who or how many were around me or if anyone was rushing over to help. It didn't matter where my mind was going or how fast it could process this situation because a few seconds later I felt an even more tremendous amount of pain from my left elbow. I heard the biggest popping or should I say the cracking sound that echoed in my ears. Not sure which one pulled it off, I was in too much pain to see who, but one of them stomped on my left elbow so hard I found out later from the Doctor that they fractured it in three places. Blood continued to pour out of my head. The pain grew, and somehow I tried again, harder than ever before to push myself off the ground. Yet, it wasn't over. Not even close. My breathing continued to get more and shallower as time ticked on. The blood never stopped. Every chance I thought it was over I was wrong. At this point, I was barely up. I managed to brace myself weakly on my knees only using my right hand. The left was in too much pain. Startled and shaking. Pondering for a slight moment I thought the attack was done. Nope, according to witness accounts, two of them teamed up and stomped on the back end of my left knee to put the icing on the cake. Now, you're probably thinking, *what the hell!* Right? It's crazy; it's bloody crazy, no pun intended. During what seemed like a long time even though it was merely minutes all I could hear myself say inside was the following, *I don't want to die, I don't want to die, not today, please not today.* I didn't want to die that day. I was a nobody with nothing, not a single piece of a legacy to leave behind. There are really no words I can say about what happened next. Maybe it was God's will or God's plan for me that makes me question everything that on that day or on that very occasion. It was like I was given a second chance. A new wind of breath came upon me. Somehow, some way I got up. I got up on my feet. Barely standing, one leg that was ready to collapse, fractured left elbow and blood draining out of my head I was up, standing. Surprised? Yeah, me too, and so were the four nice guys standing around me wondering, *what the hell, how is this dude standing?* One of the guys lurched towards my wrist to grab my watch again. At least he tried. No idea how, but I swung the pointed end of my elbow forward and knocked him across his jaw dead on. He fell back. The other three stood there petrified, stunned, dumbfounded, whatever word you want to associate the situation with they were very still. I didn't wait I shifted around and high tailed it. I never looked back, nor did I care my leg was about to give in at any second. One turn around the corner at the back end of the mall luck blessed me to find an ambulance attending to some other drug addict. The crew stared at me with the same eyes, *what the hell?* I remember the one male paramedics asking me, *"Are you okay?"* I replied after touching the wound on my forehead, pulling down my hand and staring at the pool of blood in my palm, *"I don't think so."*

Life began after that moment. I failed at different opportunities, but without failure, there is no success. First I ran my own Photography business here in Canada and partnered with a longtime friend in Atlanta, Georgia, USA. Then we parted ways and I ventured onto my own book publishing company, Bookaholic Publishing. To date, I have written and illustrated nine children's picture books and one collection of horror stories for adults. Now I run my own financial services business with at the time of writing this book my fiancé, Liza Villa.

Why? Because my life was on the line that day. My dreams never got started and I made a promise to myself when I went home from the hospital that I will not die without leaving a legacy. Even the Doctor said I was "*lucky to be alive.*" Luck has nothing to do with it.

Stop wasting your time, because tomorrow may never come. Do you want to die with nothing? Or do you want to die knowing you made life the best it could possibly be? It is time to change and evolve into the greatest version of yourself to live the life you deserve.

"Life is like a chess game – you don't want to waste a move."

Bing Gordon.

Stop being a bloody Pawn in life and start being the rightful highly respected King or Queen of Life.

Time to Evolve.

CHAPTER ONE
WHAT IS YOUR WHY?

"When you find your why, you find a way to make it happen." – *Eric Thomas*

Why do you wake up every morning? *Why* do you go to work on time? *Why* do you work-out? *Why* do you go to church every Sunday? *Why* do you do the things you do? *Why* are you reading this book or listening to this on audio? What is your *why*? What makes you want to bust your ass and be better than everyone else?

Think long, think deep, think very, very hard, and let me ask you again. What is your *why*? *Why* are you reading this book? *Why* do you want to change your life? *Why* do you want to work harder to rise above everyone else? Is it your kids? Is it your spouse? Is it your siblings? Is it your Mom or your Dad? Is it your Grandparents? Is it to live the lavish lifestyle? Is it to save for retirement? Is it to buy a house? What is your bloody *why* cupcake? You cannot move past this chapter unless you have a *why*. Don't tell me *"its money"*, that is a bunch of nonsense. *Why* money, for what, go deeper, I know there is a deeper *why*, it is time to really acknowledge it.

Think long, think deep, think very, very hard, because with no *Why* you have no purpose in life. It is harsh, but very true, indeed. If you need a little help with finding your *why* take a good hard long, yes I said long look in the mirror. Stare at yourself and ask yourself *why* you take on battles when everyone else doubts you. *Why* you fight for what is important to you when no one else cares. *Why* you continue to fail, but still honestly deep inside believe there is success coming around the corner. Stop picking your nose or scratching your ass and think about your *why*. Close your eyes if need be. Write down one, two or even three or more *why's*, no one said you needed just one. We are in this together. Your success is my success. My whole purpose of this book is to make sure you are on the right track to unbelievable success in your life. So, get with it and choose your *why* already. It is important. You are important. Make your *why* count for the rest of your life. Of course, if you have one disregard all this yapping, but if you don't, get with the bloody program already sunshine!!

Your *why* are your motivation, your ambition, your burning desire, your tears, your blood, your sweat, your butterflies, and every failure and every success you plan to have. From this moment forward I want you to hustle for your *why*. Bust your ass for your *why*. Shed tears for your *why*. Fight for your *why*. Win for your *why*. Challenge the status quo for your *why*. Fail for your *why*, yes, fail for your *why*. Without failure, there is no learning and there is no victory until you fail. I want you to take risks for your *why*. I want you to wake up every god-fearing day and say *I am going to change my life for (insert your why)*. Say it every day until you truly believe it. Cherish your *why*. Never give up and never even think about quitting for your *why*.

"Think long, think deep, think very, very hard, and let me ask you again. What is your why?"

There is a reason you finally picked that *why*. Your soul, spirit, heart and burning desire has truly connected to it. Your *why* is important and it doesn't deserve to be screwed around with. Hustle all day every day and never dare to try once in a while. Your *why* is for you to fight like it is your very last second, minute, hour, day, week, month or year on this earth. Your *why* should drive you to limitations that you didn't think possible. Why, because it's the most important thing to ever happen to you. Don't show up sometimes. Don't show up part-time. Show up every moment you get a chance to. Seek that new adventure to take you on an unforgiven journey that will change your life for the better. Why, because it is worth it. So damn worth it and you know it. Stop biting your lip overthinking things. Stop hesitating. Get with it and start living the life you deserve. Pick up your gloves. Throw a few jabs and uppercuts. Fight for your *why* and put your best foot forward to make it to the top. Make it to the top at whatever you do to make it possible for you and your *why* to live the life you both deserve.

Let's slow down and think about your idol, whoever it may be. Do you think they made it to the top of their craft because it was fun? Absolutely not. Do you think they quit when times were hard or obstacles got thrown into their faces? NO! How do I know that, because they wouldn't be your idol, you would not know who the hell they were if they gave up. Think of Walt Disney for a second. If you haven't heard the story of how he grew his empire to the next level you are in for a treat. A lot of people do not know that Walt Disney wasn't happy about his studio at the time. In 1955 He initially thought he had lost control of his dream. His ultimate dream was to open up a theme park to grow his empire even bigger. Yes, he wanted his creations or better known as animated cartoons to come alive. He wanted every child to enjoy them like he originally intended, but he wanted more. Did he fail to get what he wanted, yes, yes he did. Did he give up, oh, hell no! Unable to secure a large enough bank loan after trying bank after bank after bank after bank, yes your big banks. Walt was tired, frustrated, drained, and unhappy mentally and physically. He finally took matters into his own hands. Walt Disney borrowed against the *cash value* from his life insurance policy by Transamerica Companies. *Wait, Life Insurance saved Walt Disney?* You got it. It helped him finance the creation of his new theme park, Disneyland and the rest is history. He had a why. To him, it was his dream. He took baby steps to get his cartoons or animations to the TV screens across the world. Yes, there were trials and errors, but he had a dream to change cartoons forever. His dream then became bigger. Did he settle because he already achieved a little success? No! He took his why and did everything humanly possible to fight every obstacle in his way until he got what he wanted. Never use your why as an excuse. Never, ever use it as an excuse. Don't be that guy that questions him or herself,

"Why did they get success and I didn't?"

Be the champion that hustled and grinded every damn day for your *why*.

No one in this world deserves the success you are longing for more than you do. The time is now. Prove yourself to this unforgiven cruel world we live in. Rise above all and take the planet Earth by surprise. Naysayers, haters, screw them. This is your life, not theirs. Stop trying to please everyone else and start using your *why* to better yourself.

List your Why below:

____

____

____

____

____

Let's do this. Keep reading my friend, my comrade, my sister, my brother. Your journey has just begun.

CHAPTER TWO
STOP WITH THE EXCUSES

"Ninety-nine percent of the failures come from people who have the habit of making excuses."-
George Washington Carver

I may be aging myself here, but have you ever watched an episode of Charlie Brown and hear when the little guy speaks to adults and they reply? Well, all you hear is ***"Blah, Blah, Blah…"*** Why do I bring this up, well, the excuses that come out of your mouth, yes, your mouth sound exactly like that, ***"Blah, Blah, Blah…"***

Leaders do not daydream about excuses; they wake up, show up and lift up others around them. Your ability to change your habits is limited only by the true belief in yourself to better your life. No one is going to come and open the doors for you and say, ***this is your best life.*** You have to be willing to put your best foot forward 200% of the time. No excuses, no bullshit. Excuses of any sort will ultimately turn your dreams into dust. Excuses are a waste of space, waste of time and a waste of your efforts. The habits you create around coming up with the next excuse becomes a way of life and that way of life is complete utter bullshit. Spend that exact time, effort, creativity and resources to create habits of success instead. It takes a true leader to stand out from the crowd. To fight through any element that blocks their path to achieving what they truly want to accomplish in life or in business. Excuses will always be there, however, opportunities will not be. If you are sick and tired of hearing people around you make excuses then it is time for you to stop fucking making them too.

"Excuses of any sort will ultimately turn your dreams into dust."

Eminem said it perfectly on his song intro, Lose Yourself, *"Look, if you had one shot or one opportunity to seize everything you ever wanted in one moment would you capture it or just let it slip?"*

If you want to be the greatest, yes, the greatest leader you can achieve to be you have to stop, completely stop with the excuses. *"Oh I am late because of (Insert stupid reason here).."* No one gives a damn, show up on time and be relentless in your pursuit.

It starts with controlling your time. Make it a habit to embrace time instead of fighting it. You cannot expect anyone to allow you to lead them if you cannot control your essence of timing. You have probably heard this before, but I am going to say it again, be the first to arrive and the last to leave. If someone that is below you or on your team shows up before you and stays on their hustle longer then you, you have no right to wear the title of leader. Time waits for nobody. Whatever excuse you are brewing up inside that dead space of a brain of yours is not worth it if you truly want to make your life better or the best it can be. Whoever said *"I'll do it tomorrow..”* has never begun to change their lives, don’t be that couch riding misfit. Lead by example. Excuses come and go, but in all reality, your future depends on you.

I don’t care, she doesn’t care, he doesn’t care, and we don’t care about your excuses. Nobody is going to embrace you as they do to a champion, a winner or a leader because you are lazy. If you want to build or lead an empire of people to success stop using excuses as nails because it will only build a house of failure. Excuses do not pay bills only results do. Excuses are undoubtedly useless. Taking action is the price any great leader will have no problem paying to get the results they truly desire. Always wake up with a smile knowing that today you are going to change your life by stopping yourself from spitting out excuses. This is your time and today is day one. Take full responsibility in your life or in business or both. It is your promise, duty, necessity, and trust in yourself to take full no excuses responsibility in what you do moving forward. If it is imperative for you, you will find a way. If not, you will always revert to an excuse. The day is today to stop being a clown and start making an effort to change your life. Excuses will always be there, but is it truly worth it to you to keep using them? No, it is not. Excuses do not change lives they delay them. Burn the excuses, bury them and never think about using another one.

Today, tomorrow, next week, next month or next year I want you to start saying,

"Fuck excuses, I am taking action.."

Success occurs when your actions get bigger than your excuses. If you lose your excuses you start achieving great results. If you want more success and less stress stop with the excuses, it's that simple.

Which excuses did you use this week?:

____

____

____

____

____

Fill in the blanks:

Excuses of any sort will ultimately turn your dreams into

________________________.

Your ability to change your habits is limited only by the true ____________________________ to better your life.

It is your ___________, ___________, ___________, and ___________ in yourself to take full no excuses responsibility in what you do moving forward.

Chapter Three
Never Quit

"I never Lose. Either I win or learn" – Nelson Mandela

It will be hard. It will suck. You will fail. People will not believe in you. Your friends will turn their back on you. Life isn't easy. Winning isn't easy. Becoming the best version of you isn't easy. Getting to the top is not easy.

Never quit. I repeat, never quit!

No one has ever told you to never quit have they? No, contrary to popular belief a lot of people we trust and love will tell us we are *wasting our time*. To quit dreaming, and that dreams are for fools, and there are days you will believe all. Don't you dare, not even for a little bit. Get that thought out of your head. Do you think I wanted to be stabbed in the head, beaten to near death and just stop fighting because a couple of assholes wanted my watch? No! Absolutely not. I was twenty years old lying face down on the concrete and my soul spoke to me saying, *Derek, you're not dying today!* So, my friend, today, let your soul speak to you louder than any hater or naysayer and rise above them all. Quitters complain. Quitters criticize. Quitters will be the first ones to say, *"Oh you're wasting your time."* Or *"Don't quit your day job."* Or *"What scam did you get yourself into this time?"* Or my all-time favorite, *"Is that a Pyramid Scheme?"*

Quitters are the ones that never took risks or challenged themselves mentally or physically or at all. With all due respect, okay, maybe not, but you should never, ever, listen to a broke person. It may sound harsh, but broke people have no right to talk shit about anyone's dreams. Why, because they gave up and quit on themselves. No one has the power to shit on your dreams unless you let them. Yes, you will fail, yes, you may slow down at times, but never quit on what you truly want. You are special. You are unique. You were put on this earth for a reason. Now is the time to show us all what you're made out of. Cowards never start. The Weak never finish and the winners never quit. Now, tell me, which one are you? You best be a damn winner if you have read this far. Pain, obstacles, hardships, bullshit, fake friends, plastic smiles are all temporary, but quitting lasts forever, don't be that person.

"Cowards never start. The Weak never finish and the winners never quit. Now, tell me, which one are you?"

Let me take you back to the good old days. Do you remember when you were a baby; yes a crying, chubby, cute, pooping and peeing every couple hour's baby? I want you to remember when you first started to walk. How often did you stumble, how often did you tumble, how often did you fall down smack on your face and how often did you get back up? Exactly, too many to count, I want you to think about this, why did we never give up on a task that was so damn hard for our own good at that age? Yet, we give up within minutes, hours, days, weeks or months the moment we encounter an obstacle, a hater, a loved one that tells us we can't do it. Why, because society has molded our minds to be a bunch of over sensitive good for nothing human beings. Why did we push ourselves to speak when we were young, yet a simple thing like a comment on social media stops us dead in our tracks. You must remember to never stop trying. Never stop believing in what you truly want. Never give up, because your day will come and when it does it will feel like a rebirth of your soul living once more.

Have you ever felt defeated? Keep your head up. Someday, everything will make perfect sense. Today, you may feel like kicking the bucket and throwing in the towel. Don't, I promise you if you continue to evolve when you are having the craziest day and you feel like shit, your wins will be ten times more worth it. Smile at the confusion, keep that poker face through the tears and keep reminding yourself that you are here for a reason. What defines a King or a Queen is not that win or the victory, but the rising after the defeat. Keeping your head held high when life challenges you are inevitable, quitting, however, is optional. The pain, the tears, the suffering, the happiness, the joy, the failures and successes today are the strength you feel tomorrow. Never give up. Never surrender. This is your life. This is your dream, what happened to that mindset that you had when you were a baby? It is time to bring it back and take the world by its balls and squeeze them hard, really hard until you get what belongs to you. Financial freedom is yours for the taking, and the time is now to start taking action. Being drained is often a temporary mental block. Quitting is what makes it a reality. Don't let your reality suffer anymore. Get that thought out of your head and never let it return.

Let me share a little something with you. One of my friends once made me repeat these simple yet effective words to a group of a hundred people, *"No matter what happens I declare to never quit on my dreams."* I can honestly truly believe something was in the air as two weeks later my oldest son, Damien, age eight at the time wrote me a note randomly and left it on my desk, *"Dad, never give up, we love you."* Signed Dame & Dash. He signed in from his little brother as well. Today, I want you to repeat after me until you believe it through in through.

"My life is my life, my dreams are my dreams and I swear today, tomorrow or any day of the week that I (Insert your full name) will not quit!"

Say it again,

"My life is my life, my dreams are my dreams and I swear today, tomorrow or any day of the week that I (Insert your full name) will not quit!"

One more time,

"My life is my life, my dreams are my dreams and I swear today, tomorrow or any day of the week that I (Insert your full name) will not quit!"

Good, great, awesome, you are on the right track.

How do you feel?

Are you ready for what's next?

Your journey is looking great, keep moving forward and never stop to look back and never quit. You got this.

Fill in the blanks:

__________ at the confusion, keep that _____________ through the tears and keep reminding yourself that *you are here for a reason.*

Keeping your head _________________ when life challenges you are ____________, _________, however, is optional.

Chapter Four Get Committed & Stay Committed

"Most people fail, not because of lack of desire, but, because of lack of commitment." – *Vince Lombardi*

Unless a commitment is engraved in your soul, there are only broken promises and false dreams, but no plan of action. You cannot control your empire; you cannot control your life unless you are 110% committed.

Motivation is what gets the fuel burning. Commitment is what keeps your dream or goals alive. With undeniable commitment, it leads you to unbelievable action which brings closer to the life you are fighting for. You do or you don't, there is no in-between. The choice is yours. Two roads to walk down, which one are you going to choose?

"I'm committed" or,

"I'll do it tomorrow."

Don't listen to the bullshit statistic when they say, *don't be greedy*, screw that, this is your life, get committed and be greedy in what you want and what you desire in life. Commitment means waking up every day and pushing yourself when no one else is around. The road ahead may get ugly, it may suck, it may cause bumps and bruises in all the right places, but the results will be beautiful, that I promise. Shortcuts are for the weak. There are no shortcuts when you are all in. Every one of us was dealt a hand of cards when we were born. God didn't give you the roughest upbringing if he didn't see something special in you. He wanted to test you to bring out the greatest most passionate version of yourself. People like you and I that learn the value of hard work, commitment, hustle, and sacrifice are the ones that make their lives great. Don't cheat on your life. Don't cheat on your *why*. Don't cheat on your dreams. Don't cheat on your goals because the second you do your commitment goes out the window. Bye, bye commitment. Commitment is that turning point in your life when you seize the moment to alter your destiny. Always remember, if you are not scared you are doing it wrong. I want you to demand yourself to excellence and to victory. When you take massive actions towards your dreams, you must trust yourself to figure out how to create it one step at a time and adjust your path as you go. Commitment equals activity and that activity should never be seen as a setback. Never regret anything. Remember with any obstacle or situation that holds you back that came from your journey towards your final goal are there to learn from. You never failed, you just took another path to learn and make you wiser, stronger and better than you once were. Never, never, never give up, things never happen by accident. They happen because you have a clear vision. You, my friend, have a deep desire and commitment to live a great life. If you commit to something you better be ready to prove it. Because commitment is not a noun to be defined, but a verb to be acted upon and when you are truly committed you to do whatever it takes to get your hustle on. Stay on track and keep focused because your journey will lead to greatness. If you do one thing today, make sure you do something that will make you better tomorrow. Commitment is the sum of small, medium and large efforts, duplicated day in and day out. It is not about having the knowledge or skill to do something. It's about having the will, passion, desire, ambition and commitment to do your very best. Non-stop until you get to the top. Change your mindset, change the way you think, change your day-to-day actions and I guarantee you'll be one step closer to achieving your goals and dreams. Commitment is the superglue that seals you to your goals. Push yourself because no one else is going to do it for you. Strive for success because there will always be someone that is right behind you trying to do the same.

"If you do one thing today, make sure you do something that will make you better tomorrow."

If you are working a 9 to 5 job, stop working on another man's dreams and start the committing towards yours. JOB = Just Over Broke. Think hard, think long, think deep and very, very long. If you are currently working at a JOB, how often are you free? Free to arrive when you want to arrive without being disciplined? Free to take breaks when you want to take a break? Be paid what you want to be paid? You work so hard to have your hard cold cash go out the window the second it comes in. You need to be aware of the 40-40-40 scam that plagues JOB's worldwide. Why work for 40 hours a week for 40 years to only receive 40% of your monthly income because your boss or employer thinks less of you. Retirement is a scary thing. Inflation is a horrible thing. Stop working on someone else's dream and start becoming committed towards your dreams.

BOSS = Bully Over Successful Students. Successful Students is exactly who we are. We win, we fail, we tumble, we fall and we get back up wanting more. Why, because in our minds we love the risks, the challenge, the bumps, the bruises, the long nights, the early mornings, and everything single aspect involved in chasing our dreams. Because we are the ones that never give up, we never give up. We want the better life. You want the better life. No dream is too small, too big, or too unbelievable because entrepreneurs never quit. We stay committed to what we desire in life. Commitment needs goals. Aspire to make a difference with your dreams and life. Ignore the opinions of broke people. Stick to your goals. Bring your dreams to life. Share your journey with the world. Work hard. Fall forward. Learn from your mistakes and keep going until your last breath. Picture in your mind at all times the future you want, the future you desire, the future you are fighting for and not wait any longer to take action. Just because 90% of people do not make it, doesn't mean you can't.

You are an entrepreneur and entrepreneur's never quit.

Fill in the blanks:

What does JOB mean:______________________________
What does BOSS stand for:__________________________

____

What is the 40-40-40 Scam:________________________

____

____

____

CHAPTER FIVE
DRESS THE PART

"Always dress like you are going to see your worst enemy." – Kimora Lee Simmons

There is nothing more embarrassing than showing up looking like a slob. Start dressing the part, and time to be honest with yourself starting today. Do you truly believe your first impression is your lasting impression? If the tiny voice in your head answered *yes*, then it is time to change your wardrobe.

Believe it or not, I have seen people show up for corporate overviews or open-houses looking like they just came in from playing a game of pick-up basketball. With a backward cap, long oversized t-shirt and baggy wrinkled jeans on, unbelievable to say the least. This is possibly the future life presenting it that you've been longing for and you show up like a damn slob. Like you just rolled out of bed and put little to no thought in how you present yourself. Do you really think for one tiny millisecond the business world, your clients or anyone, in general, is going to take you seriously? NO! First, you get up, then you dress up and then you show up. Let me repeat that. First, you get up, then you dress up and then you show up. Anyone serious in this world when it comes to business sees you like that, a slob, it doesn't matter what master's degree or work experience you may have, deep down inside we are laughing at you. You bet your ass we are judging you. What did you expect; this is the real world after all. Don't give me the bullshit comment,

"I dress how I feel comfortable…"

Great, awesome, just don't bother wasting your time or anyone else's time when you look like a damn teenager working at a fast-food joint.

Never underestimate the power of dressing up. Everyone and I mean this from the bottom of my old ticking heart will judge you, so why not let them judge you the right way. Dressing good, dressing sharp is a form of mental power you have on the world. If you look good, you feel good and you bet that ass of yours you'll produce good results in life and or in business. Dressing up doesn't mean you spend all the money you have, no; you can go to thrift stores to find great things for great prices. Don't spend money you don't have until you have it. No this isn't *fake it until you make it*. This is I need to look good so I can start from the bottom and rise and grind until I get to the top. Looking good gives you the confidence to do anything you set your mind to. I wish I knew this when I was younger, don't blow the only opportunity you may have because you decided to show up like a bloody slob. The moment you take care of yourself is the same exact moment the world starts caring for you.

"Looking good gives you the confidence to do anything you set your mind to."

Are you tired of feeling like a shadow in the crowd? Great, maybe it is time for a change. Change the way you look. Sharpen up that hair dew, shave that beard, touch up that makeup and start looking presentable. Don't whine, bitch and moan when you didn't get the shot at your dream job or career or your clients walked out because you came looking like you rolled out of bed. In the world, in general, we see thousands of people walk through the doors you just did. What is going to make you stand out from the next pawn in the crowd? Don't tell me your smile, your eyes, your work ethic, because you know and I know that is the biggest bullshit filler answer we all heard and all used millions of times before. Back in the early years of my business, I remember being told I was going to speak in front of a room of a hundred people. When I showed up wearing dress pants and a company polo shirt I was denied from speaking with no explanation. Apparently, I didn't get the hint, the next time I didn't show up looking a hundred present. One of my friends and mentors told me, *"I wanted you to speak, you got the suit down, the shoes down, but you forgot the tie, come on man."* In my mind, I was like, *"What the fuck, it's a damn tie."* It takes 110% before you gain a foot forward to success. Get with the program and wake up early, dress up totally and show up like you damn well own the place. I had a story to tell that would have inspired those hundred business-minded individuals that showed up to listen. Unfortunately, I was like you and didn't think my appearance mattered. However, the guy at the time that did much less then I accomplished got the shot to speak because he woke up early, dressed up totally and showed up like a champ.

Listen, this is important, don't show up stinking like a pig either. We understand you may not believe in perfume or cologne, but cover up that awful body odor. There is nothing worse than a fine dressed man or woman showing up stinking like they haven't showered in weeks. *Damn, Derek, this is common sense.* Apparently not, welcome to the business world. We encounter this way too much. Respect yourself, respect others, dress up, show up and hustle until your day comes.

Fill in the blanks:

Do you really think for one tiny millisecond the business world, your clients or anyone in general is going to take you serious? NO! First, _______________, then _______________ and then _________________. Let me repeat that. First, _______________, then __________________ and then ___________________.

The moment you _________________________________ is the same exact moment the world starts ____.

CHAPTER SIX
SET UNREALISTIC GOALS

"The Victory of success is half won when one gains the habit of setting and achieving goals." – Og Mandino

What in the hell is this guy talking about? Set unrealistic goals, this guy is bloody crazy, why am I even reading this book? Did I guess it right; was that the first thought or question to pop in your head when you read the title of the 6th chapter? Great, because I meant it, it is time to start setting unrealistic goals.

First, we went through why it is important to have a generic reason *why*. Second, I spoke about never quitting, and now we are going to jump right in and talk about setting unrealistic goals. I am just going to put this out there, the more hustle you put towards your goals, the greater you'll feel when you achieve it. Forget these tiny little goals anyone can achieve with their eyes closed. Your goals moving forward should scare the hell out of you, but excite you a lot. You'll never change your life if you don't max-out your goal setting. You're not going to change yourself if you continue to make tiny little goals. The real value of creating high unrealistic goals is not for appreciation or compensation, it's the person we become by finding the will, tenacity, and hustle to produce them. You can see yourself evolve at a faster rate when you challenge yourself.

Never stay quiet about your goals. Tell everyone, why, it

holds you accountable. It makes you go at them ten times more because you told everyone. Don't be shy about your dreams. Picture this, you set a goal to start a business and you don't tell anyone. That business starts taking off, what do you think will happen? Your business will fail because you decided not to be proud of your goals. Be proud, set goals and speak loudly about them. Not just once, not twice, but every moment you get a chance to. If you want that promotion at work, talk about it. If you want to start your own business, talk about. If you want to own your own house one day, pick one out and then talk about it. We all have dreams in this wonderful world of ours, so why not let the whole planet know we are gunning your way towards them. What would you love more, clapping for yourself or have all of your family, friends, and associations clapping for you? Exactly, make the world aware of who you are and what you are about to achieve and I guarantee the mindset that cooks up inside will push you father then you could ever imagine before. Keep your eyes focused. Your mind opens to doing whatever it takes to get your goal completed. Get your heart pumping faster, and yell out,

"Game Time!" every time you set out in full force action to achieve your goals.

The trick to achieving any goal is to constantly keep your eyes on it. Sounds strange, but it is true, 100% true. How you may ask, *how in the world can we constantly keep our eyes on our goals?* Sticky notes are awesome, social media posts are grand, however, if you have a picture of the goal you'd like to achieve or own, print it out and hang it on the mirror, the fridge, at your job or your business. Take at good lengthy look at it every morning, lunchtime, dinnertime and every opportunity you possibly can.

"What would you love more, clapping for yourself or have all of your family, friends, and associations clapping for you?"

Here are some tips that will help you achieve what you want in life. First, grab a notebook, place it next to your bedside. Second, after waking up from your slumber open that notebook, date it, write your number one goal and below that write three ways you are going to achieve that goal today or three ways to get closer to your goal today. This stimulates your brain to constantly think about your goals or dreams during the entire dawn-to-dark adventure you have daily. When the sunsets and you hop back into bed, review your goals, see what you achieved and what you failed at. No excuses needed. Don't cry. Don't whine. Write your main goal down again if you did not achieve it that day and write down what steps you did achieve. Get a nice red or black marker and cross out the steps you achieved. Never write them again, ever. The next morning, write down your main goal, and of course the steps you never carried out and then write new ones. Keep moving forward. Never look back. If you keep doing this, day-in and day-out, observing your goals, reviewing them and hustle until your heartbeat stops, and then hustle a little bit more because you know deep inside you want that goal more than anyone else. I guarantee you will come out on top.

What about setting unrealistic goals?

Hold yourself at the highest standard possible. Reach for the sky, then through the clouds and then right into outer space. *Huh?* Grant Cardone said it best when he said the following,

"10 Times the actions, 10 times the goals & you'll get everything you ever dreamed of."

I want you to feel ambitious and passionate about everything you do. Setting goals are as important as breathing. If you want massive results, change the amount of action you plan to take. If you are in the sales business and your daily goal is ten sales a day, change it to one hundred. You have to amplify your goals. Your unrealistic goal of one hundred sales a day will probably never happen. However, your mindset is now set to achieve the unachievable. Your ten sales will go to double or triple if you continue to place that goal day after day in writing and repeat it in your head. Think about this for a moment. If you set that one goal to ten times more the actual amount and you achieve fifty percent of it, are you successful or a failure? You're bloody successful champ. Not only did you blow away your original goal, but you 5x it. Be proud if you double it. Never get off your grind once the goal is set. Actions always speak louder than words ever can. Set goals. Talk about them. Double, triple, ten times your original goal and get outside, believe you can do it and you can my friend. Your goals are initially what provide food on your plate. Stay hungry because it will ensure you and your *why* don't starve. Never, ever lower your goals, increase the steps you take to achieve them. Sacrifice everything you can to become the better version of yourself.

The whole understanding of unrealistic goals is simply maxing out small goals. If you often set small goals to try and double it, triple it and go beyond your limits to maximize your results, nothing is greater than achieving a goal you never thought possible.

Write down your top three goals:

___

___

___

___

___

___

___

___

___

___

___

CHAPTER SEVEN
BECOME FEARLESS

"The question isn't who is going to let me; it's who is going to stop me." – Ayn Rand

Once you become fearless life becomes truly possible. Your only limit is you. Escape the comfort zone and change your life. Always remember this, if you fear the world you fear the person you are rightfully are meant to become.

Even in your darkest hour, day, week, month or year the sunshine inside will rise again. The power to fear anything is all in your head. My basketball coach in Grade Six and Seven, Randy Wallace taught the team,

"no matter where you play, inside, outside, the park or the gym, your opponent(s) doesn't know anything about you. That fear that floats around in your head, is just that, in your head. Keep focused on what you do best and destroy your competition. They do not know you, but make sure by the end of the game they remember you."

As powerful as it may sound, it is very true, indeed. Never doubt yourself. The moment you do that is when fear creeps in and overtakes your ability to think straight.

Trust your gut and don't think, just act. If you let that little voice in your head think or yap on before you take action the deadly thing you and I call fear will take over.

Do you want to know what puts fear in people's minds? Success. The moment you start making moves and attempting to climb up the ladder, everybody that you call a friend, co-worker or associate will hate you because you are now competition. The greatest fear we face in the world is of the opinions of others. Not only does it kill our self-esteem, it kills our motivation to do better. The moment you are unafraid of the opinions of others that truly do not matter at all, you are no longer a Pawn in the Chest game. You become a Rook. Then once one conquers the realm of average you become a Knight on a mission to success. The fight for freedom and the chance to become a Bishop, however, the main aim is to become Queen or King of your life and it is closer than you think.

What is a Pawn: a pawn is a person that quits at everything the moment the slightest or tiniest obstacle gets in the way. They love telling you to quit and say you are wasting your time. Yet, they have never really started living their own lives. First to judge, last to compliment, do you know any Pawns in your life? My advice, distance yourself.

What is a Rooks: No better than a Pawn, however, they have taken some risks. Tiny risks, but nothing major to get out of their comfort zones. Rooks are the type to talk shit and gossip about everyone else badly, yet when it is time for them to get a taste of their own medicine they lose their mind. They are satisfied with a 9 to 5 job. They fear to lose stability. Same advice, distance yourself from Rooks.

What is a Knight: Knights are fighters, they always think about living a better life. They try and position themselves in situations that don't really do anything for them. They tend to have fifty, fifty success and failure rate. They have a lot of passion and ambition, but never a game plan nor a desire to take it to the next level without the help of others. Learn from Knights, but never copy them.

What is a Bishop: They are always hungry for success. They take risks, big, medium and small ones. They take chances when everyone else is scared to. They have the desire, passion, ambition nearly 24/7. They take action and have an entrepreneur mindset. They are rare if you meet one if you are not one yourself, use every valuable second to learn from them.

What is a Queen or King: They are fearless. They are the one man or woman that everyone loves to hate, why, because they take huge risks, and fight every day to get out and stay out of their comfort zones. They don't hesitate. They just take massive action to stay on top. They are the ultimate Hustler. The Champion, the one that never stops learning nor never stops failing. They believe that with every failure there are lessons to learn from. Success is always in their grasps because they don't take shit from no one.

The moment you surround yourself with the right type of individuals, the moment you become fearless. The thoughts you put in your mind, the people you surround yourself in and the environment you are constantly in will shape you. If you hang around with a bunch of Pawns or Rooks, you are bound for failure. However, if you surround yourself with the right Knights and Bishops you are bound for success and a whole lot trial and error. Trial and errors that lead to success and the ultimate greatest version of yourself that you've been waiting for. Take a good look in the mirror and ask yourself,

Fear the world or have the world fear me?

You are your only competition, nothing else matters.

Wake up every morning and say this until you believe it,

"This is my life, this is my world, I control it. I fear nothing. Fear is just a word. I am greater than fear. This is my life and I control it."

Fear is just a word, take a look, it means, an unpleasant **emotion** caused by the **belief** that someone or something is dangerous, likely to cause pain or a threat.

Become Fearless!

List the people you consider Pawns and Rooks:

Now, do yourself a huge favor and figure out a way to get them out of your life as soon as possible. Better your surroundings and you'll better your life.

CHAPTER EIGHT
YOU MUST HAVE GRIT

"Grit is the grain of character. It may generally be described as heroism materialized, - spirit and will thrust into heart, brain, and backbone, so as to form part of the physical substance of the man." – **Edwin Percy Whipple**

Grit has nothing to do with your smile, your College or University Degree, your leadership, your ability to be awesome or even your talent. You can be the most talented person in the room, but I promise you it will not guarantee you will evolve in this world.

Grit is not meant to standalone, you must have passion alongside with it. Passion will get you from point A to B during your journey to evolve correctly. Passion is what we all bloody have, it's not just passion that makes up Grit, Grit is passion, perseverance and commitment mixed into one. Grit helps you leverage the pursuit of perseverance in overcoming obstacles over an extended time frame. The passion mixed in makes the journey feel less like work and more about the outcome and how you feel daily, weekly, monthly and yearly. With no passion your journey to become the greatest version of yourself is just BLAH!!! Grit is nothing to take for granted. Grit reflects an individual's long-term commitments to goals and life in general. It is not just a made up word. It is part of your mindset and mental attitude you have towards yourself and your life. It is your assessment of obstacles of any sort that fall into your path. Grit goes beyond the average mind or individual. You are not average. Average people have fixed mindsets and have difficulty thinking outside the box. Fixed mindsets will subconsciously hold you back.

You as the greatest version of yourself must always remember there are no limitations, no walls and nothing holding you back, but yourself. Open up your mind, see beyond the imaginary walls, step out of your comfort zone and get rid of your self-limitations. If you can dream it you can achieve it. You have the skills, intelligence and capability to evolve into anything you put your mind to. Grit is something we all have in us. We know deep down there is no stopping us from any adversity or challenge. You must believe and conquer anything and anyone that stands in front of you, especially your mindset. Think positive rather than negative. It is your right to evolve and grow. It is your right to clear your life and mindset from negativity and live the great life.

"Open up your mind, see beyond the imaginary walls, step out of your comfort zone and get rid of your self-limitations."

You cannot be uptight or stiff like a board. Be flexible and innovative. If things do not go as planned don't do the average thing and get frustrated over dumb shit, keep calm and keep moving forward. Never believe if you fail once that it is over, be optimistic and proactively look for solutions. Surround yourself with like-minded individuals. Create a culture of success and growth. Imagine if you surround yourself with other people with the passion and perseverance that you have and continue to grow and evolve together how powerful you all will become. I cannot stress it enough when I say this, get rid of the negative influences in your life once and for all. It does nothing but hold you back, avoid envy and jealousy. Think outside the box. Strive to fail, focus on growth rather than failure. Believe, achieve and strive to win-win not just by yourself, but with others as well. Be proactive on your pursuit to evolve into the greatest version of yourself.

Grit isn't about getting your hands dirty. It is about putting everything you have in you on the table at any given point and if it doesn't work for whatever reason you don't give up, you keep going on and on and on no matter what. Day one begins with you, are you ready to evolve?

Answer the question below:

1. Do you have a high drive full of passion?

____

____

2. Are you ready to commit to your dreams and goals?

____

____

3. What is perseverance and do you have it in you?

____

____

____

Chapter Nine
Control Your Thoughts

"Every thought we think is creating our future." –
Louise Hay

Negative vs. Positive Thoughts and how bad or how good do they affect you daily, you may not be aware of it, but negative thoughts have the capability to bring catastrophically negative obstacles, individuals and situations into our lives.

Wait! There is good news when you switch the negative with the positive you can mold those negative individuals, obstacles and situations into positive ones, which will bring forth more abundance than you can imagine. Let me ask you, have you ever had days where you couldn't wait to get home and once there you just felt emotionally drained? How about working so hard and not being appreciated by your boss or loved one? Illness, depressed or have fatigue? How about putting in all the overtime and busting your ass to make your business or side gig pay off and all you ended up with was another failure?

Contrary to popular belief, every mental, physical, emotional state of unhappiness you encounter is on you. It's not my fault, his or her fault that you are not succeeding at something. The stone cold truth is you attract everything that happens or the people and situations around you by the thoughts you think. The law of attraction works like this. It is all about the vibrations in and around you. Let off negative vibrations, thoughts, words, etc. and negative will follow. Don't blame me, don't blame anyone else but yourself because at the end of the day it is you who is causing it. Switch gears and start thinking and acting in a positive matter and positive things will come back your way. If you fail at something do not sit there and grumble, strategize on ways to perfect the next time or come up with a new solution in a positive matter rather than all-out quitting. If you are broke or want more money make it happen. Think positive and money will come to you. Let me add, it is not just positive thinking that will get you money in mass amounts, you must take action too. Rome wasn't built in a day and neither will be evolving into the greatest version of yourself. Take steps, one by one and stop thinking, talking or doing negative things and your life will start to blossom. There is always sunshine after the storm. The time is now where you make sure there are no more storms brewing. Positivity will bring you to places that you couldn't imagine possible.

Chances are you find yourself thinking about the past, I understand why, but you must keep your eyes on the present and goals for the future. We can't change the past. No one can. Stop dwelling on it. You can't go back. Live today, forget about yesterday and plan for tomorrow. If you find yourself slipping it is important you have your goals at arm's reach. Your brain will try and fill your head with images of the past, but simply say to yourself as you hold up your goals,

"That was a great time, but let's focus on my future."

I'll share this personal story in hopes it inspires you. I was raised by a single Mom with three other siblings. I never knew my Dad and it never held me back. Yes, I admit, it would have been a blessing to have him there growing up, but I never dwelled on it. At an early age, I made a promise to myself if I was to ever have kids I'd make sure they'd have me in their lives. Why, because I took a negative and made it into a positive. I never for one-second thought, *oh I never had a Dad so I'll never have kids.* Being a Father has been the greatest blessing of my life. Changing the way you think will change the way you live your life and who you become in the long run. Just because your friend had a failed marriage doesn't mean you will. Just because you had a horrible upbringing doesn't mean you will make your child go through the same thing. Positive thinking can change the outcome of anything. Any obstacle, any thought or any situation will prevail with positive thinking any day.

"There is always sunshine after the storm. The time is now where you make sure there are no more storms brewing."

I'll share one more thing about my upbringing to hopes it

motivates you further. My Mom did her best to raise us, feed us, clothes us, unfortunately, drugs got the best of her at times. As a young child, I saw the toll it took on her and kept my distance from drugs. My Mom never had a lot of extra money; most of her money went on household things, food, and drugs. We never got the fancy things in life. You can say we were below average. God bless her for trying to do her best, but she fell victim to the 9-5 lifestyle and never wanted anything more. I never understood why, but I knew I had to keep positive and keep growing as a man because one day I'd be in this world alone eventually. With the Law of Attraction and Positive thinking, I've created a legacy beyond the 9-5 lifestyle. The financial business I mentioned at the beginning of the book can and will be passed down to my children and their children's children to come. The royalties from my book sales will continue to come in and go straight to my children/family. Why, because positive thinking, grit, confidence, perseverance and taking action made me the man I am today and just like you if you follow through you can evolve into something great and something beautiful. Control your thoughts don't let your thoughts control you. Live life to the fullest and understand you control everything. The decisions you make, the thoughts you ponder are all because of you.

List five things that you are grateful for right now:

1.____

____

2.____

____

3.____

____

4.____

____

5.____

____

List three friends you enjoy being around:

1.________________________

2.________________________

3.________________________

List four places that make you happy:

1.____________________________________

2.____________________________________

3.____________________________________

4.____________________________________

If you completed the assignment and filled out five things you are grateful for, three friends that you enjoy being around and four places that make you happy you are on the right track. Take those friends to those places and share with them the things you are grateful for, and you will see a positive environment bloom.

CHAPTER TEN
TAKE ACTION – GET LUCKY

"Take action! An inch of movement will bring you closer to your goals than a mile of intention." – *Steve Maraboli*

Do you believe in magic? Serious question, do you believe in magic? Quick answer, don't. It is all smoke and mirrors, but the old saying I do believe in is *"The harder I work, the luckier I get."* And you should too.

There are two types of action, do nothing or take mass amounts of action. I want you to acknowledge that our lives are the efforts we put into it. Good people do not get lucky because they are simply good. Good people are blessed with the lifestyle they are currently living because they took the right amount of action to get there. They put in the discipline and sacrifices needed to evolve into the better version of themselves, not once did they wake up seeking the sofa or hid under the blankets waiting for life to blossom for them. They took action to achieve greatness. Michael Jordan, Kobe Bryant, and LeBron James all had dreams to make it to the NBA just like a lot of other kids growing up. The only difference between those kids and Michael Jordan, Kobe Bryant, and LeBron James are they took massive amounts of action to make it to the NBA. They learned discipline, commitment and took their passion, grit and stuck with it. Early morning practices, practices after the and before practices. Training Camps, late nights over and over throughout the years, these three gents are known as the greatest that ever played the game because they didn't settle for anything less than great. They knew deep down that dreaming would only get them to the couch or the backyard to play pick-up games, but they knew through and through that hard work and taking that extra amount of action will one day change their lives forever.

What are you going to do today to get you to the next step in your journey and the next step after that to keep evolving? It is time to start waking up early, exercising not just your body, but your brain as well, and take some small, medium or big type of actions towards your goals. Let the average sit on the couch and watch Netflix while you are fighting, sacrificing, waking up early, going to bed early as nothing happens good after 9:00 pm and working towards your ultimate lifestyle change. Taking action is one thing, but the most successful people take care of themselves mentally, and physically, why? Because if you look great you feel great you can bet every dollar in your pocket you produce great results and attract positive abundance in your life. Prioritize what is important and never waste time on anything else. Never hide behind an excuse as it will only hold you back and if you do it once you'll repeat it over and over again. One step today is one step closer to the greatest version of yourself and the greatest life you have ever lived.

"Let the average sit on the couch and watch Netflix while you are fighting, sacrificing, waking up early, going to bed early as nothing happens good

after 9:00 pm and working towards your ultimate lifestyle change."

Today is the day you must make a list of things or people to put to death. No, you are not becoming a hitman, but you have to kill relationships starting today. Think about people that always talk negative or only talk to you to complain, kill it. Kill anything or anyone that only brings negativity to your life. Pull out the cord, end the lifeline and walk far-far away. If they do not support you on day one they are not going to support you in the future. Keep your eyes on the bigger picture, the future, the better stronger version of yourself and nothing else. Yes, it may be uncomfortable, but today is the day you get comfortable being uncomfortable as there is no turning back. You must always remember you must take action consistently daily even if it is a small action. You'll never succeed if you only act when you feel good. It doesn't matter if you are sicker than a dog, broke your arm or just feel like having a lazy day. One day can change your whole situation. Slow down, but never stop. Johann Wolfgang Von Goethe once said, *"Sometimes our fate resembles a fruit tree in winter. Who would think that those branches would turn green again and blossom, but we hope it, we know it."* Keep in mind if you see no results today it doesn't mean the person you are today isn't preparing to evolve tomorrow. Keep going and remain focused on what really matters to you. Stay true to who you are, be grateful for what you currently have, but always stay hungry for more.

I'll share with you a personal experience that is the definition of proof that taking action is worth every shot given. Back in Grade Seven of Elementary School poetry was the hardest thing for me. I couldn't rhyme any words to save my life. I actually received a D for not completing the poetry assignments given that year and I felt like shit. I remember to this day we had to write a poem about a dragon and we were told to hand it to the classmate directly in front of us. The teacher called upon my classmate to read mine out and his answer has haunted me to this day,

"I am not reading this, it doesn't make sense and it doesn't even rhyme."

The class burst out in laughter. However, yes the situation was depressing and most would never try again I didn't let it stop me from evolving. To date, I have written, illustrated and published nine children's picture books in rhyming format. Three of those books have been on Amazon's Best Sellers list, two at the exact same time. I've sold books across the globe and received amazing reviews because I never gave up and took action to go beyond my comfort zone.

Action is yours to take. You were born ready, start today.

How much time did you spend watching Netflix this week?______________________________________

How much time did you spend working on yourself or your ultimate goal?______________________________

If question number one is higher than question number two you need to do some serious thinking, however, if question number two is higher, you my friend are on the right track. There is nothing wrong with relaxing, but it should never outweigh evolving.

Chapter Eleven
Be So Good They Cannot Ignore You

"Creativity is inventing, experimenting, growing, taking risks, breaking rules, making mistakes and having fun." – *Mary Lou Cook.*

Today is the day for a new beginning. If you want to evolve you have to master it. Be so good they cannot ignore you any longer. By the end of this book which is very close I want your community, your whole organization, your whole city to know your name. However, I cannot create that, you must. Today is day one and you've been selected to come aboard to the big leagues. The door to average has closed for good.

Today is the day you swear to yourself and the heavens above that you will not quit until you get the results that you want. You will not quit until everyone knows your name. You will not quit until you've built the biggest sexist legacy that no one can touch for hundreds of years to come. What brought you to this point today will not be enough to carry you past tomorrow. You must keep learning, evolving and building yourself up for the greater good. Evolving to the next level will not happen if you do not master what you are currently doing. You need to be so good at your current craft that there is only one name your boss, your church, your community, your industry calls your name first when they need what you do. I cannot tell you what to do to get better and what you do. The only person that knows how to get better at your craft is you. Write a list of things you need to accomplish in order to move on to the next level. With each step on the list, there should be three goals beneath it. These goals will help you to succeed. Never doubt your goals. Remain confident and keep at it until your fingernails bleed or your toes break from all the hard work and dedication you are about to put forth. Don't be skeptical when it comes to bettering yourself, the only skeptical people in the world are broke. Those are the same people who tell you to quit when times are looking good for you because of cold hard jealousy and envy. If you want a chance in evolving into the greatest version of yourself you have to go all in. Hold nothing back. You deserve nothing more than you fight for.

"The door to average has closed for good."

Paying your dues and doing your time is not just for individuals in prison it is for you and anyone else looking to master their lifestyle or craft. I want you to understand in full context that the best part of being the greatest version of yourself is not being a clone to society but being your true self. Nothing worth living is easy and being too good to ignore is a blessing in itself. Strength comes with struggle and I know if you are reading this book you have struggled. You have lost sleep. You have begun to wonder why this world is so cruel and most of all you are looking to change the world around you. Step by step, action by action, big or small you are on your way. The path you walk today is only temporary as long as you never give up on what you truly want. Stop living life poor, hungry and dissatisfied. Your *why* needs you to keep evolving. Stop saying,

"One day, one day, one day I'll make a change."

Do it today. You were born to do something significant in this world, you can do it, and we all can do it. Life is like a blank notebook, God created the first page and the last page, whatever you do in between is up to you. It doesn't matter if obstacles hit you right in the face, keep standing strong and keep moving forward. If your *why* doesn't inspire you anymore commit to a new one. You have to have an unshakeable belief in yourself to achieve your greatest dreams, you got this. Hold yourself to great standards. Elevate everything you are currently doing, change everything you are doing and you'll evolve in no time.

The million dollar secret to living the greatest life ever is simply *hard work*, are you ready to put in the work?

Write a list of things you need to accomplish to move onto the next level:

____

____

Goal:____

____

____

Goal:____

____

____

Goal:____

____

____

CHAPTER TWELVE
DON'T BE AVERAGE BE OBSESSED

"Stop being average. You're not even good. You were born to be great." – *Eric Thomas*

If you want to be one of the greats you have to become obsessed with your craft, your abilities, your talents, your gifts, your goals and most of all you have to be obsessed in evolving into the greatest version of yourself.

Tough times do not last only tough people do. Your name, your brand is your reputation so why the hell are you letting everyone see you as average. If you want to be the best singer you need to be obsessed with becoming a great singer. If you want to be the greatest salesman in the world then you need to be obsessed. Walk the walk and talk to talk. No holdbacks. Don't treat your life with the average mentality. Treat it like you are the damn King or Queen of your industry. Stop walking like you have a stick up your ass. Start walking like you own the damn place. If you don't own it yet be obsessed and figure out how to own the place. Life is real. You don't have an eraser to cover up your mistakes. Fail, get up, fail, get up, repeat, retry and keep at it until drop dead. Breathe your craft; eat your craft, dream about your craft, practice, practice, practice. Make every moment count. No one ever remembers number two. Never settle for second place.

Figure out your strengths and your weaknesses. Be obsessed in building up your weaknesses until they out due your strength and then switch. Evolve, evolve, evolve and evolve again. The ultimate source of success is an obsession. Do you think Michael Jordan became the greatest to ever play the game of Basketball because he settled for average? NO! Do you think Rap Icon Tupac Shakur is known across the world because he settled for average? NO! He has released more music since he has passed away then he did when he was alive. Why, because he was so obsessed with making music and getting his message out there he made it his duty to be in the studio every possible moment he could. The best thing you can do for yourself is to have self-belief. Don't just say or claim you are the best at your craft be obsessed and prove it. Leave your ego at the door. If you don't stop moving forward you'll be pushed/pulled back to ordinary.

You are who you are for a reason. No one claps for the ordinary person. They don't applaud for average. They only applaud and cheer when you put your best foot forward. Challenge yourself each and every day that you are awake to push yourself to be or to achieve better in whatever you do. I want to challenge you to not be the victim and nothing less than the greatest version of yourself each and every day. Live life on your terms; be obsessed for your future. Your decisions determine your destiny. Never compete. Dominate at every corner. Expect it to be difficult. Welcome the struggles. Nothing worth fighting for comes easy. When passion meets inspiration, an obsession is born. Are you ready to be reborn? I know you have that burning desire, that roaring passion and inspiration just waiting for you to ignite it. Set the fire ablaze. Get to work. Move your ass. Start that hustle. Open up your eyes. Obsess. Obsession is essential to creativity. It is the water in your lake. The lava in your volcano, the red on your rose, and without obsession life is nothing. Don't live to die, live to live the life worth living. Be obsessed with your drive, your desire, your commitment, your why and most of all be obsessed in evolving to the next level to success. The next level of your life, the best level of your life, your mission now is to allow your obsession to overpower any doubt in which may remain and become to best you can be. Let people think you are crazy. Let people state the obvious and say you are obsessed. Obsessed is the word broke and lazy people use to describe dedicated people like you.

"Determination becomes an obsession and then it becomes all that matters." – Jeremy Irvine.

Let obsession consume your mind because it will put you on the right track to control your life. Train like your obsessed. Eat like a nutritionist, sleep like a baby and win like a champion. Stay hungry. Stay obsessed. It's the only thing that will ensure you don't go broke and go hungry. There is no shortage of winning in this world keep bringing the heat. Never lower your obsessions increase your actions. You were not born to be average or do a good job. You are here to make a difference in your life and the lives around you. Anyone who thinks you are crazy or tells you to stop gunning it towards your dreams is either not a real friend or very confused. Your greatness is limited only by the efforts, goals, and steps you take to improve yourself. A failure is never an option. If you are not already you should be obsessed with winning and winning only.

"No one claps for the ordinary person. They don't applaud for average."

Bonus:
Red Light Syndrome

For a moment I want you to think about life and how it is like a red light at any given intersection. Red lights equal to obstacles or situations that just come out of nowhere. We all hate red lights. They stop us from getting to our destinations and delay us when we are in a hurry. Think about the last time you left your place five minutes later than usual. I bet you felt like you hit every stop light imaginal. I guarantee it frustrated and annoyed you after the third or fourth one and the thought of, *I am definitely going to be late now,* crossed your mind. Red lights are just like life. If you procrastinate, delay or believe if you do it tomorrow you'll get the same results, sorry, you're wrong. I want you to understand this; red lights do not last forever. If you take action towards bettering yourself today rather than tomorrow you'll hit fewer red lights then if you delay or procrastinate and wait for even five minutes more.

Red lights or better known as obstacles are not meant to stop you, you always have options once you roll up to a red light. You can fight time and wait to move forward, you can plan ahead and be in the right turning lane and have the option to turn to go around the light/obstacle or you can simply let it stop you dead in your tracks.

Red means stop, but two seconds later Green means go. Are you going to stop forever due to one red light/obstacle or are you ready to live life in the Fastlane?

Thank you for reading my book I hope it inspired you as much as it inspired me writing it, if anything in this book motivated you or changed your life please leave a review on Amazon it would be greatly appreciated.

You are meant for greatness and the time is now to shine like the diamond you were born to be. Good luck and enjoy life to the fullest.

Cheers,

Derek J. Kenmuir

www.ingramcontent.com/pod-product-compliance
Ingram Content Group UK Ltd.
Pitfield, Milton Keynes, MK11 3LW, UK
UKHW041849190726
13854UKWH00002B/794